ROMANIA

TRAVEL GUIDE

A GUIDEBOOK TO THIS

FASCINATING COUNTRY

BY

RYAN MILLER

Table of Contents

An Introduction to Romania

Nestled in the middle of the colder regions of southeastern Europe, Romania has often been called the central country in Europe due to its strategic location in the center of the Central, Eastern, and Southeastern European countries. Bordering the Black Sea, one of the most mysterious bodies of water on its Southeastern border, Romania has a unique foundation on which to plant its tourism industry. Additionally, the rich heritage of its surrounding countries such as Bulgaria, Hungary, Ukraine, Serbia, and Moldova makes Romania one of the most diverse countries in Europe. Romania's climate varies around a temperate-continental climate that keeps the country relatively cold year-round. When compared with its fellow members of the European Union, Romania comes in within the upper 50 percentile, settling for 8th largest country by land mass and supported by the 6th most populous citizenry of the countries. In all, over 20 million citizens call Romania home, aiding the workforce for a country that is among the smaller countries of the world. Much of Romania's folk-lore and industry utilizes the Danube River, which is the second-longest river in Europe. This river brings many countries to Romania, beginning in Germany and tracing its way through numerous European countries before finally reaching its destination, the Danube Delta in Romania. Adding to the mysterious and cold front of Romania, the Carpathian Mountains are among Romania's most beautiful sites, a site that regularly commands most of the tourism industry's attention. The Carpathian Mountains bow to the peak of the mountain system, the Moldoveanu Peak, which pierces the sky at an astounding 8,346 feet.

Romanian history has different segments, all demanding that proper respect and identification be made. The most popular and recent segment of Romanian history started in 1859 when the country was founded, the result of a union that brought the Danubian Principalities together from their respective territories in Moldavia and Wallachia. Romania received its name in 1866 and followed this with its independence in 1877. One of the more confusing moments in Romania's history came in 1916 with the emergence of the first world war. While Romania initially maintained its neutrality neutral during the war, it aligned with the Allied Powers and upheld their allegiance; however, in May 1918, the Treaty of Bucharest followed the Central Power invasion of Romania, subsequently causing Romania to enter the world war on November 10, 1918. Following the war, Romania added Bukovina, Bessarabia, Transylvania, Banat, Crisana, and Maramures to its borders. These countries together became officially known as the Kingdom of Romania. These years marked the height of the Romania government's extension and in 1940, the Molotov-Ribbentrop Pact was coupled with the Second Vienna Award to demand that Romania give Bessarabia and Northern Bukovina to the growing Soviet Union. Additionally, Northern Transylvania was ceded to Hungary. This pact led to a bitter rivalry between Romania and the Soviet Union, setting the stage for Romania to fight against the Soviet Union in World War II, thus joining sides with the Axis. Romania's affect in the war did not prove to be substantial and the country was even permitted to switch allegiances, joining the Allies only after the country recovered its portion of Northern Transylvania from Hungary.

World War II had the single-most greatest affect on the outcome of Romania's history as the Red Army entered the country following the war. With the Red Army maintaining residency in the country, Romania officially aligned as a socialist republic and solidified this identification by joining the Warsaw Pact. This form of government proved most unsuitable for the Romanian people and the frustrations of the people culminated in the 1989 Revolution. The Romanian government listened to its citizens and removed its alignment as a socialist republic and began shifting its government towards becoming a democracy run on the engine of the market economy.

Today, Romania's government has been recognized for the poor development of its people, the country actively recognized as 52nd on the table of Human Development Index. It is regarded as a developing country, an economy that in emergence, has worked its way to the 47th largest economy globally by nominal GDP. In 2017, Romania was recognized as the fastest growing economy in the European Union with 7% annual growth. Romania's economy is substantiated by the presence of the service industry, its best-performing industry. The chief business operations of Romania center on machines or electric energy. Romania was not among the founding countries of the United Nations but did join the coalition five years after it was founded in 1945. In 2004, Romania joined the North American Treaty Organization (NATO) as added protection for its balance on trade. The decision to join the European Union was not one that took place overnight. The country had been primarily in favor of joining the European Union but full integration did not occur until 2007. Romania was first introduced to the European Union in 1993 when it applied for membership. Two years later, the country was issued Associate status, aligning Romania as an Associate State of the European Union. Nine years later, Romania's strong economic position made it one of the leading European countries and its diligence was rewarded with an upgrade to Acceding Country. Finally, Romania achieved status as a Full Member when its living standard for the country greatly improved from 2005-2006.

Romania has not been immune to global recessions, most recently going through a recession during the late 2000s at the same time in which the United States saw the housing market collapse. During the global recession of 2008, Romania was forced to borrow money from the International Monetary Fund. While most of the world saw the recession lead to growth from 2012 on, Romania's weak infrastructure allowed the financial crisis to lead to a political crisis, which led to deep corruption in the sectors of medical services, education, and local government. Romania righted the ship in 2013 with higher wages and lower unemployment, all leading to *The Economist*'s declaration that Romania was once again considered a "booming economy." Today, Romania is surging on the Human Development Index and boasts of an economy that both supports the citizens while allowing strong government growth.

An Introduction to Romanian Tourism

Tourism is among the most important parts of the Romanian economy, netting almost 5% of the country's gross domestic product. From quaint villages to beautiful mountains, Romania is one of the newest contributors to the world's tourism sector; however, it is also one of the fastest-growing tourism sectors in the world. The World Travel and Tourism Council has high praise for Romania's tourism, noting that the country is currently experiencing the fourth-fastest growing tourism industry in the world. This same study found that the country's tourism industry is experiencing almost 8% growth yearly. This is of utmost pertinence to tourists thinking about touring Romania since often, the most toured locations in the world find their credence in their high and growing number of tourists. In 2016, the country saw an unprecedented 9.4 million tourists, the majority visiting during the summer months when hiking the mountains is most enjoyable. While the immediate influence of the tourists is felt through lodging, souvenir purchases, and tour guides, the non-immediate yet directly influenced categories of growth involved in Romanian tourism included investments made into the tourism sector. Romanian tourism saw investments totaling €400 million during the 2005 tourism season.

Most of Romania's tourism comes from directly adjacent countries, with additional tourists coming from fellow countries in the European Union. As noted earlier, the border of the Black Sea adds tremendous influence to the Romanian tourism industry. With resorts such as Mamaia dotting the Black Sea coastline, Romania is seeing an increased number of tourists coming to Romania strictly for the sea-side resorts. With beach resorts dominating summer tourism, the winter months are largely visited by tourists in search of some of the most thrilling hills in the world. With ski resorts open yearly in the mountains of Romania and others that thrive on the seasonal weather afforded their portion of the country, skiing is Romania's second-highest grossing tourism sector. Romania's ski resorts are unique in that they often border sights such as castles and seas, giving tourists a view while skiing they will rarely find elsewhere. Some of the most popular tourist attractions for skiing are found around the Valea Prahovei.

Tourists to Romania will find that the country caters heavily to tourists so they can be certain of having a pleasant time. The recent emphasis the world has placed on tourism has led many Romanian tourist agencies to increase the standards by which they rate attractions, leading to an increased standard of living for tourists. Today, tourists to Romania will find a full host of activities. The beauty of Romania has led to thousands of tourists returning year after year and is certain to meet the expectations of all tourists entering the country.

The Culture of Romania

The emphasis of this section of the tour guide will be on the numerous holidays on the Romanian calendar. This information is applicable and pertinent to tourists since the demand for hotels, food, and travel accommodations will increase around many of these holidays. Additionally, some of the holidays lead to chaotic times around Romania, chaos that tourists will most likely want to avoid. Listed below are the holidays, what span of days they are celebrated, and the origin of the holiday regarding whether or not it is nationally celebrated or a simple cultural celebration.

January 1-2: New Years Day

Following the culture of the rest of the world, New Years Day is celebrated on the first day of the new year and celebrations usually last for one day following the actual holiday. When this holiday falls on a weekend, it is not rare for the celebrations to seep into the next week as well. Tourists visiting Romania for the sites and not necessarily the culture will want to avoid this time of year most attractions will be closed. All necessary institutions such as hotels, gas stations, and some restaurants will remain open.

January 24: United Principalities Day

This holiday is an official non-working holiday celebrated nationally to commemorate the famous unification of the Roman Principalities from Wallachia and Moldavia that occurred in 1859. With this day regarded as the day that Romania officially became a state, it is celebrated as Romania's independence day and most businesses will take off several days for celebration. Because the day hinges on the cultural independence of the country, tourists are encouraged to avoid visiting during this time unless they have family in the area or will recognize the cultural displays of the holiday.

February 19: Brâncusi Day

This day is set aside to commemorate the life of Constantin Brâncusi, a famous Romanian sculptor and painter. With most of his work accepted as modern art, this man is now regarded as the patriarch of the modern sculpture movement. While Romania reveres this man and is proud to hail his patronage within the country, this is not an official day off of work and not a public holiday. Tourists will find very little disruption within the country and should be fine to visit during this holiday. Additionally, many art museums will have public displays on this day dedicated to Brâncusi's works, giving tourists and citizens alike the privilege of seeing his work on display.

MARCH 8: WOMEN'S DAY

Though not a public holiday, this day is set aside to commemorate and celebrate the accomplishments of women, past and present. While some organizations might close to honor the women of the organization, all public tourist attractions remain open and there is little disruption to the public travel flow. Tourists should expect some street closures for public demonstrations of gratitude to women but these street closures usually have clearly outlined traffic detours.

FINAL SUNDAY IN MARCH: EARTH HOUR

On the last Sunday of March, a worldwide practice called Earth Hour has found its way to Romania, with businesses and residents encouraged to turn off all non-essential items that require electricity. Those observing this holiday are encouraged to turn off such devices from 8:30-9:30 pm. This is not a public holiday and is primarily observed on the residential platform. Tourists should expect no disruptions during this holiday.

First Sunday in April: NATO Day

NATO Day is celebrated on the first Sunday of every April to commemorate the alliance's reach into the trade agreements of its member's countries. This is not a public holiday but every government organization will observe the holiday. There are no closures for this holiday and its observance is typically relegated to a celebration at key government buildings. Tourists do not need to avoid the country during this time.

Easter

Tourists will want to pay close attention to the observance of Easter the year they are planning to tour Romania. Romania is a devout Eastern Orthodox country, with much of the country practicing Orthodox Catholicism. With the Easter holiday changing exact days from year to year, tourists will want to consult the calendar prior to making traveling plans. This is an official public holiday in Romania and most businesses and attractions will remain closed for its duration. Also included in this holiday is Good Friday. Known culturally as Pastele, Easter is considered the second-most important holiday in Romania and hundreds of cultural celebrations take place throughout the weekend. Tourists should avoid traveling to Romania during this holiday.

May 1: Labour Day

An international holiday set aside to celebrate the accomplishments of the labor unions of the world, Labour Day (Labor Day) is a public holiday celebrated on May 1 across the world with the exception of the United States and Canada which celebrate the holiday on the first Monday of September. This holiday is considered a break from work for almost every business and most public attractions close to observe its elements. While all travel agencies, airports, hotels, gas stations, and some restaurants will remain open, tourists will find little more to do in the country on this day and with domestic travel increased on this day, tourists should avoid traveling to Romania round this holiday.

May 9: Independence Day

This holiday is celebrated throughout all of Europe, in Romania as Independence Day and throughout Europe as Victory Day or Europe Day. This holiday is set aside to commemorate the day that Romania proclaimed its independence from the Ottoman Empire following the war with the Ottoman Empire in 1878. Because Romania had already been established as a country, this day is not synonymous with Romanian liberation. Because England experienced its own victory from the Nazis in 1945, effectively ending World War II, this day is also celebrated as Victory Day. Until 2007,

Romania did not observe this holiday; however, with its admission to the European Union, Romania has since observed both Victory Day and Europe Day on May 9, effectively celebrating three holidays on one day. While these holidays are significant, they are not considered public holidays and therefore, few businesses will close their doors. While some historical and political institutions will hold special rallies or speech demonstrations, there is little disruption to the traffic and business plan of the country and tourists are at liberty to tour the country with little frustration during this holiday.

MAY 10: KING'S DAY

This holiday honors the medieval period of the Romanian government when kings and queens ruled the Romanian people. Specifically, it is celebrated to commemorate the crowning of Carol I as the first king of Romania; however, numerous other kings and queens also are remembered on this day. Because it is not a public holiday, there is little disruption to travel and business transactions. Tourists can expect to see some celebrations at history museums or monuments but should be fine to travel the country with little delay.

40th day from Orthodox Easter: Heroes' Day/Ascension

This holiday is celebrated exactly 40 days from the observance of Easter. Though not considered a public holiday, is tremendously important to the Romanian people since most are devout Orthodox Catholics. Since the holiday centers on the religious market of Romania, tourists are encouraged to avoid traveling through Romania on this day. If tourists are in Romania on this holiday, they can expect to see numerous public celebrations and some religious parades. This is one of the holidays that even tourists with no affiliation to the Eastern Orthodox religion will find interesting.

June 1: Children's Day

This holiday has been observed globally since its inception in Geneva in 1925; however, its observance in Romania as a public holiday is young, first being observed in 2017. This holiday is a day set aside to celebrate the children and is usually celebrated globally on November 20; however, Romania has set aside June 1 as the day the country will celebrate children. With it being a public holiday, numerous businesses will close and tourists should expect delays to the travel pattern as parades are commonplace. Even though it is observed as a national holiday, tourist attractions should remain open and sometimes, tourist attractions will even offer free admission to children. Tourists will enjoy the cultural representation on display during this holiday and should not avoid traveling to Romania during this time solely because of Children's Day.

June 7: Pentecost/Whit Monday

Following the habit of the other Catholic holidays of the country, this holiday falls on the 50th day following the celebration of Easter in Romania. Similar to the other Easter holidays, this holiday is celebrated on different days every year. In 2020, it will be on June 7 and 8. This holiday is considered a non-working holiday and is celebrated nationally. Tourists are advised to avoid traveling to Romania during this time due to heightened travel arrangements domestically. Most hotels will be completely full months in advance. Tourists with family in the area might enjoy the cultural expressions celebrated during this time; however, most tourists will be frustrated by the lack of accommodations available during this time.

June 26: National Flag Day

This holiday is not considered a public holiday and very little celebration surrounds it. As a day set aside to commemorate the beauty of the Romanian flag, there is not much celebration and people maintain their typical daily routines during this time. Three days later, the

Romanians celebrate National Anthem Day, a commemoration of the first time that the Romanian anthem was played in 1848. Tourists are welcome to tour Romania during this time and will see little more than heightened patriotism and nationalism on these two days.

AUGUST 15: DORMITION OF THE MOTHER OF GOD

As tourists most likely realize by now, many of the national holidays within Romania are centered on the Eastern Orthodox Religion and the Dormition of the Mother of God is no exception. This holiday is set aside to celebrate the Mother of God and her ascent into Heaven after being resurrected following her death. This holiday is usually commemorated with a large feast, much dancing, and days of fellowship. Tourists with no affiliation to family in Romania or the Eastern Orthodox religion should avoid touring Romania during this holiday. This holiday takes on pertinence with the naval forces since St. Mary is considered the patron saint of the Navy.

AUGUST 23: LIBERATION FROM FASCIST OCCUPATION DAY

This holiday holds a special connection to World War II and is unique in that it is actually a retired holiday.

From 1949 until 1990, this day was celebrated to commemorate the numerous individuals present during King Michael I's coup against the Conductor of Romania, effectively aligning the country with the Allies during the World War. Additionally, the day is now celebrated as the official holiday of the European Day for Commemoration of the Victims of Totalitarian and Authoritarian Regimes. Finally, this day is also reserved to remember the famous Molotov-Ribbentrop Pact that initially ruled that Romania would lose its territories now located in Moldova and Ukraine. This is not considered a national holiday and little of this day is celebrated. Tourists should see no disruptions to their tourism during this holiday.

December 25: Christmas Day

The final holiday that tourists should be concerned with is Christmas Day. This holiday is celebrated culturally but contains the same reverence as the rest of the world places on this day. Tourists might find the country beautiful at this time of year but should be prepared for numerous tourist attractions to be closed both for seasonal reasons and the holiday.

Now that tourists have an idea of the prime times to visit Romania, a brief look at the culture of the country will allow them to interpret some of the nuances of the people. Perhaps the most dominant trait of Romanian culture is the adherence to folklore despite its age. Most of the Romanian culture is thousands of years old, with traditions such as wood carvings, ceramics, weaving, and embroidery garnering the attention of households across the country. Today, while many of these habits are considered cultural, there are entire museums dedicated to the folklore of the country, the Museum of the Romanian Peasant and the Romanian Academy being the most well-known. With most of the country containing large forests, wood has been the primary building component for hundreds of years. Houses, gates, and windmills were constructed of heavy slabs of wood, many of which remain to this day. For the clothing of the people, linen has remained the popular fabric. During the winter months, the locals will pair the linen with wool to maintain warmth. Tourists to the country will notice the dominance of the color black on the clothing; however, some locals branch out and use colors such as red and blue depending on the culture. The common attire for men is pants, a white shirt, and a thick leather belt that is usually hand-crafted. Often, men will also wear vests over their shirts. To better navigate the hilly territory, most men wear long leather boots or shoes made of leather. These leather shoes are referred to as opanci. The final piece of clothing that men wear is a hat that often denotes the region of the country from which the man hales. Each region maintains its own distinctive design, a design for which the men of that region are proud. The women of

Romania often wear white skirts accompanied by matching shirts and vests. Unless attending a religious function or a formal social function, the women will also wear an apron that is referred to as a sort or a catrinta. During religious functions, it is not uncommon for the outfits of the women to be quite flamboyant.

The Romanian culture remains structured around the dance and music that have been a part of Romanian lives since the country was born. The music of the country demonstrates the influence of neighboring countries. Additionally, the most popular music of the country is sad, melancholy music that tells the sad stories of Romanian upbringings. Though Romania's culture may be quite different than a tourist's culture, tourists should rest assured that the culture of Romania is very inviting and friendly. Romanians often invite tourists to join them in celebration and dancing, leaving tourists with a part of the culture and a happy memory to remember their time in Romania.

THE ATTRACTIVE CITIES OF

ROMANIA

Certainly, tourists to Romania will be far more interested in the natural landmarks of the country than merely touring the cities; however, Romania has beautiful cities that deserve at least a night's lodging and exploration. The following section will focus on some of Romania's more beautiful and unknown cities. This is not an exhaustive selection but this list will show tourists cities to at least consider staying in during their vacation.

TIMISOARA

Tourists will love the city of Timisoara, a city known for its quaint yet modern beauty. Located among numerous rail lines, Timisoara is a perfect destination to spend the night during a rail-line trip. Many tourists have noted that new tourists could comfortably spend a day exploring the city's stone architecture and still not see everything the city has to offer. While in Timisoara, tourists are encouraged to take advantage of one of the famous sightseeing tours guided by professional tour guides. Additionally, there is another tour that many tourists have raved about: the Timisoara: Grand Communism Tour. This tour sheds light on the negatives affects World War II had on the city, showing tourists the darker side of Romanian history. Along those same lines, the Timisoara: Jewish Heritage Walking Tour will leave tourists with a greater respect for the people of Romania and the hardships they endured so many years ago. While in this city, tourists are encouraged to take advantage of the benefits of the Revolut Bank Card so that they can avoid carrying cash and avoid paying fees at any of the many ATMs in the city. Tourists merely desiring to lodge in the city overnight will find The Houstel to be the most recommended hotel that is friendly to a budget. Tourists looking for more luxurious accommodations but do not want to pay a large sum for such arrangements will find the Savoy Hotel much to their liking. Finally, tourists prepared to spend money on some of the finest luxury in Romania will be delighted by the luxurious accommodations of the Hotel Del Corso. Though a city nestled in the Western region of Romania, Timisoara offers a slow pace for tourists while remaining a modern city.

SIBIU

This city, found in the region of Romania known as Transylvania, offers tourists a glimpse into the medieval period of Romanian history. In 2007, Sibiu was elected the cultural capital of Europe, donning some much-needed attention on the aging city. Today, Sibiu showcases both the modern advances of the country while maintaining the cultural heritage that the city was founded on thousands of years ago. In 2008, Sibiu was recognized by *Forbes* magazine when it was named the 8th Most Idyllic Place to Live, out of all of the cities of Europe. Founded in the 12th century, Sibiu evokes a small town while remaining one of Romania's largest cities. The city is divided into two sections: the Upper City and the Lower City, and true to its aesthetic appeal, these two divided sections are joined by staircases. Sibiu is a city founded on the cultural expression of its citizens, most apparent in the multi-colored houses that, while painted in atypical fashion, maintain an austere beauty that is hard to find elsewhere in Europe. Tourists to Sibiu will want to check out the famous Piata Mare, which translated, means "The Big Square." At night, this square takes on new life as local performers climb to one of the stages and being singing the country's popular music. Sibiu is home to seven castles, making it the perfect destination for tourists desiring to gain historical knowledge while in Romania.

For tourists interested in Romania's art, the famous Brukenthal Museum of Art will answer questions regarding style, artists, and era. Much of Romanian art centers on the Anatolian Carpets, masterful carpets whose quality is expressed in their existence despite their age. Related to the art of the city, Sibiu is also home to religious landmarks, the most famous being the Catholic Basilica. Sibiu' s most famous street is the Strada Nicolae Balcescu, a throughway that leads tourists from the Piata Mare to the lower city. While on the walk, tourists will be treated to the beautiful flowers, some maintained by the city in municipal flower gardens and others maintained by citizens in window boxes. Tourists have long reserved the title of "Best View" for the Council Tower whose peak pierces the sky and leaves tourists with a view of the expanse of the city and the beautifully orange-tinted roofs.

The smaller sibling to the Great Square, the Piata Mica is the famous square of the lower city, located at the bottom of the Council Tower Steps. While touring this square, tourists should visit the Pharmacy Museum, one of the country's premier museums dedicated to the medicinal advancements of the country since the medieval period. One of the most notorious landmarks of the city is the famous Bridge of Lies. Wives-tales tell of individuals hearing a creaking noise after telling a lie while standing on the bridge. Today, the bridge is considered one of the premier photo opportunities within Sibiu, a beautiful white house and red home being joined by the rustic metal bridge.

One of the final tourist attractions in Sibiu is almost as unique as the city's name: houses with eyes.

Paying homage to the ancient architecture of the country, many of the homes of the country are built with dual windows in the attic, windows that take on the appearance of eyes when seen from afar. The unique nature of Sibiu will leave tourists returning for years, the city requiring multiple visits to be completely explored.

CLUJ

The city of Cluj is important to Romania's economy in that it the country's second-largest city. Some locals refer it as Cluj-Napoca while some have shortened that name to simply, Cluj. The vibe this city is markedly a bustling metropolis yet the numerous castles cast an ancient and watchful eye. Many tourists regard Cluj as one of the most romantic cities in all of Romania, its poetic foundation found in almost every aspect of the city. In recent years, Cluj has become known for its party scene as its festivals last late into the night in a raucous demonstration of the modernization Romania is experiencing. This summer, tourists will be delighted by the Electric Castle, a festival that received the honor of being the best medium-sized festival during the 2019 European Festival Awards. With the genre of electronica slowly creeping onto the popular stage once held by classical music in Romania, the country is seeing more festivals dedicated simply to this musical genre. In the final months of the summer, the famous Untold Festival allows Romanians to hear some of the latest electronica music performed by new and veteran musicians alike. The musical foundation of Cluj is not found in the electronica genre, however; the genre that resonates with most citizens is jazz and the yearly Jazz in the Park celebration held during the last week of June attracts tourists and citizens alike. In 2019, the European Festival Awards honored the Jazz in the Park Celebration with the Best Small Festival Award.

If there is any doubt of the creative flair that Cluj demonstrates, this is dispelled with the National Art Museum of the city. In addition, the city is known for unique museums such as the underground art gallery and the Fabrica de Pensule, which demonstrate art that is unique to the country. Tourists who feast on the art and music of a country will want to be sure to visit Cluj and its dozens of music and art museums. The modern art of the world would not be complete without pointing out that one of the premier modern art galleries, the Galeria Quadro is located in this bustling artist venue. Completing the foundation of the art scene, the bars of Cluj serve some of the finest craft beers and cocktails of the country. The world-famous Joben Bistro is classified as a steampunk bar that will serve any variation of cocktail that a customer wants. Tourists attracted to the artist scene of Romania will want to attend the Insomnia Bar to catch a glimpse of one of the leading artists or musicians who also frequent the venue. Prior to being primarily a bar, the Insomnia was an art gallery that served alcoholic beverages to guests as they walked around. When the beverages of the art gallery became famous throughout the city and country, Insomnia restructured as a bar that also has an art gallery.

If this has not already been revealed by the art, music, and bar scene, it should be noted that Cluj is a refined city with luscious living quarters and beautiful gardens. Most of the natural attractions are found elsewhere but for tourists desiring the peace and quiet of luxury, this city is the perfect destination. Some have said that the most beautiful portion of the city is the Botanical Garden that is home to more than 250 different types of roses. Just across the city, the Ethnographic Park and Museum will give tourists the glimpse into Romanian culture and heritage. For tourists wanting to take some of this Romanian culture back with them, the famous Helofita is an outlet store that sells second-hand clothing at reasonable prices. Tourists who enjoy shopping for unique representations of various cultures will enjoy the shopping scene in Cluj, which provides customers the privilege of taking home luxurious Romanian goods at an affordable price. Tourists will also want to check out the famous Tabita outlet store and The Mill Handmade for Life where thousands of leather goods are available for purchase, all made by skilled Romanian craftsman.

The final element of Cluj that separates it from the other cities of Romania is its tremendous hostels. Though this is a new element to the society of Cluj, the dozens of hostels already in Cluj are among the nicest and highest-rated hostels in Europe. Tourists should consider staying at the Iron Hostel, where prices range from $20 per bed to $30 for a double. Another great hostel is the Zen Hostel with similar prices. These hostels are popular destinations for the students of the country and the affordable yet beautiful accommodations make for an enjoyable stay.

BRASOV

Tourists interested in the historical aspects of Romania, specifically, the history of Romania during the Middle Ages, will want to add Brasov to their list of cities to explore. While other cities in Romania have shed their medieval cloak for the more modern garments, Brasov remains true to its roots and is consistently one of the most toured cities. Located in the heart of Transylvania, Brasov offers tourists the ability to explore medieval Romania while maintaining modern living arrangements. Tourists should begin their journey through Brasov on the famous Piata Sfatului, or the Council Square. This location has become the unofficial heart of medieval history for Romania, the square taking on the form of an arch and almost beckoning for tourists to turn back time and see how life was hundreds of years ago. The clock tower in the middle of the square has survived since its construction in the 1200s and its constant ringing adds an aesthetic and ornate appeal to the city. A little-known fact about the Piata Sfatului is that this location was once used for executions during the medieval period of Romania's existence. Another key tourist attraction in the city is the famous Biserica Neagra, or Black Church. This church was the victim of a ravaging fire in the late 1600s, earning the church the distinct title of Black Church. Today, the church has been restored to its natural beauty; however, the ruche remains the largest Gothic church in Eastern Europe and is visited daily by thousands of tourists. Lately, the church has become a popular venue through which individuals view art from the Ottoman Empire, Hungarian Kingdom, and the Saxon influence of art.

One tourist attraction in Brasov that tourists will find more in line with the general tourism of the country is Tampa Mountain. The citizens of Brasov have adored this mountain as their own, mounting a sign with the word "Brasov" on its side to reflect the Hollywood influence. Tourists are encouraged to hike to the top of the mountain and take in the beautiful views that are only visible from the peak. To get to the top of the mountain, tourists are able to use either a cable car or hike up one of the two trails. The route to the top of the mountain is not difficult to hike but some tourists have remarked that there are enough rocks that spell disaster should one twist an ankle. Tourists are able to hike to the top of the mountain without the aid of a tour guide. The top of the mountain showcases the expanse of the entire city, giving tourists the prime photo opportunity for all of Brasov.

Not all of Brasov's beauty is visible from the mountain-top—to view some of the beauty one must walk down the streets looking down instead of up. This is because Brasov has become famous for its cobblestone streets. With cobblestone underfoot and numerous cafés dotting the roadway, tourists are able to turn back time and enter a different era of Romanian culture. These streets also provide tourists with ample photo locations, the prime time for photos is the morning. With these streets winding and cramped from both sides by stone-faced buildings built entirely adjacent to each other, tourists will feel as if they have returned to the colonial-era of Romania.

Some of the growing tourist attractions in most countries are the walking tours offered throughout the historical portions of a city. Brasov has joined this movement with numerous free walking tours that allow tourists to glean from the historical knowledge of the native tour guides. During the peak tourism season from April to September, tourists can enjoy a free walking tour every evening at 6 pm. The walking-tour guides of Romania are distinguished by an orange cap or garment. These tours last on average 2 and 1/2 hours and will take tourists through the Saxon District and the Schei District. The walking tour of Brasov has been named the Most Popular Free activity in Brasov and will keep tourists entertained for an evening.

To the rear of the famous "Brasov" sign that adorns the side of Tampa Mountain, there is a collection of towers that are affectionately known as the Black and White Towers. These towers are accessible from a walkway that has been cleared by the years and years of tourists attending the castle. The White Tower was constructed in the late 13th century and is still able to be entered. The Black Tower, though not black in nature, has a construction date that was not recorded but was recently renovated to accommodate large numbers of tourists every day. These renovations included a glass ceiling so that tourists can see the glistening night sky from one of the highest locations in Brasov. Tourists will enjoy using one of the two wooden staircases leading them from the safety of the ground to breathtaking heights. In addition to these castles, another fascinating historical site is the narrow street of Strada Sforii, which translated means the String Street. At the street's widest point, a mere 53 inches separates the buildings facing each other on the street. This street was originally designed to allow firemen the ability to cut between the buildings should there have been a fire; however, it has since become a tourist attraction and tourists will enjoy skillfully navigating their way through the narrow street.

The medieval crown of Brasov is found in Catherine's Gate, the only original medieval gate that is still standing. Made in 1559, this gate has stood the test of time and retains a Coat of Arms from Brasov prominently on its face. The gate is found between two pillars that house a collection of three turrets. With a look that belongs in a fairytale, this gate is one of the most popular photo opportunities within Brasov. In medieval days, passing underneath the three turrets was a confirmation that one identified with the authority of the Town Council and violation of any council laws could result in death. After experiencing Catherine's Gate, tourists must check out the Saint Nicholas Orthodox Church that is situated on the Piata Unirii. This beautiful church houses many mysteries, none greater than the time capsule that was discovered in the church's spire. Within this time capsule was the oldest Bible in Romania. All of these items have been placed in the church's museum, which tourists are able to visit during business hours.

While the Black and White Towers seem to command the attention of those seeking medieval history, there is something to be said about the massive structure that stands only miles away from the historical center of Brasov. The Rasnov Fortress is a stately castle built in the early 1500s. It towers over the city, one time keeping a watchful eye for those who would seek harm against the citizens of Brasov. In all, Brasov is markedly a city that is centered on preserving the medieval history that once was lived as reality in the city. Tourists will enjoy the slow pace and beautiful scenery that compliments the city's growing food and party scene.

BUCHAREST

Bucharest has become one of the leading cities that attracts artists from around the country. Known as Little Paris, Bucharest is Romania's capital city and is home to a thriving art scene in addition to numerous malls that have made it one of the most important cities to the country's economy. While Bucharest may be the capital and one of the most artistic cities in the country, the violence surrounding the city has become a serious concern for the country and, more specifically, for the tourists. All throughout the city, the numerous art museums are overshadowed by buildings that have fallen in disrepair since their tenants left for better opportunities. In the middle of neighborhoods that are falling apart are numerous churches, showcasing the religious function of the city. Today, the top tourist attractions of Bucharest include the Palace of Parliament and the Statue of Emperor Trajan. Additionally, artistic and historic lovers will enjoy the Cismigiu Garden and the Museum of the Romanian Peasant. All together, the historical attractions of Bucharest will leave tourists satisfied; however, the disrepair of buildings has begun to detract from the city. Romania has pledged to maintain the safety of its tourists, allocating additional spending to the city's renovation. Until then, tourists will get an up-close look at the true society within Romania, not one that has been covered by tourist attractions. Bucharest is a city that contains the raw beauty of the country and will keep tourists busy for days exploring art museums and simply observing the rustic beauty.

IASI

Known for its ornate rock structures, Iasi is recognized as Romania's largest city, complete with so many churches that it is known as the "City of the Hundred Churches." With monasteries accompanying the churches and squares maintaining the beating heart of the city, Iasi is the swagger and ego of Romanian cities. With a history with ancient and medieval roots, Iasi showcases the different eras of Romanian architecture, giving tourists the perfect basis for which to compare the different years of Romanian architecture. There are also numerous botanical gardens that add to the luster and beauty of the popping colors the flowers bear. The pride and joy of Iasi is the Palace of Culture, a museum considered the best in Romania. Ordained as a castle, this palace contains little historical value, its creation dating to merely 1925; however, the location of the palace is significant. The coordinates of the palace are directly over the court that Prince Alexandru cel Bun once walked back in the early 1600s. There are four museums located in this cultural hub.

One other beautiful element of Iasi that showcases the Romanian culture is the Jewish Cemetery erected as a monument to the victims of the Iron Guard, a fascist government regime alive many years ago. There are four bunkers made of concrete designed to commemorate the lives lost during this dark moment in Romanian history. Living up to the name that has dictated the success of Iasi and its religious affliction, the Church of the Three Hierarchs gives tourists the perfect spot for a picnic lunch amidst exploration. Though the largest city in Romania, Iasi remains a city focused on its people and tourists are no exception. Tourists are treated kindly and valued for the attention they bring to the city.

Constanta

A city that is vital to the export success of Romania, Constanta is Romania's largest port city and considered the most beautiful city located on the coast of the Black Sea. With the city being visited by tradesmen from different countries every year, this city captures the blend of cultures that have seeped into the country. It gives tourists the prime opportunity to see the beauty of Romanian cities while also taking advantage of the nearby Black Sea to fish or boat. This city is home to Mamaia, a resort that is largely considered the most up-scale and highest attracting resort in Romania. Constanta has paired daytime activities and a vibrant nightlife to give tourists the relaxation they need while also being transparent and giving tourists an honest view into the culture of the country. Located a short three hours away from Bucharest, Constanta gives tourists a fantastic day trip that will take them from an artistic city to an industrial one. One of the most mysterious attractions of Constanta is the famous Abandoned Casino, an odd rock structure located at the end of the Constanta Boardwalk. Once a lively casino, this structure has been repurposed many times, one time even serving as a hospital for the soldiers during war. Its most recent operations included House of Culture, where tourists were treated to a presentation on the numerous cultures of the country.

Today, it remains abandoned for its exorbitant costs needed to maintain operation.

The peak season of tourism in this Constanta is summer when thousands of tourists will flood the city for weeks. For tourists who enjoy a bustling vacation, the summer months will afford them this lifestyle; however, some tourists may enjoy the leisure pace of "normal" Romanian life and touring during the fall or winter months will afford them this lifestyle. Either way, Constanta is the unique hybrid of a working city coupled with being one of the most attractive cities for tourists.

Although this list has excluded numerous cities that a tourist would find enjoyable, these are the best cities that tourists consistently rave about when returning from a vacation to Romania. Tourists vacationing in any of the cities listed above can be certain that they are receiving the best care and attention in Romanian while seeing the Romanian culture for what it is: hospitable and hard-working.

THE DIFFERENT TOURIST ACTIVITIES OF ROMANIA

Romania is truly a country of diverse tourist interests with activities ranging from historical exploration to hiking the Carpathian Mountains. Romania's tourism industry has only recently become the major force for which it is now recognized; however, tourists should feel assured that the country has progressed quickly in making attractive accommodations and tourist attractions for its guests. In the following section, this guide will focus on the various tourist activities of Romania, with no specific attraction mentioned. The contents of this section will give tourists the peace of mind that Romania has a vast array of tourist activities to keep them busy for the duration of their vacation.

HISTORICAL SITES

While Romania's most well-known historical period came during the existence of the Soviet Republic, there are still visible signs of the country's medieval history available to tour today. With castles in almost every major city, tourists should be sure to add a castle exploration to their vacation to-do list. The castles, though no longer used today, remain in very good condition and tourists can climb to the top of many of them. The castles are a tremendous reminder to the Romanian people of how far the country's government has come. In addition to the many castles found in the country, there are also a good number of historic churches that demonstrate Romania's adherence to the Eastern Orthodox religion.

Cultural Hotels

While most of the world speeds towards modernization, Romania is one country that has chosen to remain in the century of its heritage. This heritage is seen most prevalently in the modest yet traditional accommodations found in the countryside. While large cities such as Brasov and Iasi have hotels that will luxuriously accommodate guests, the small homes in the countryside resemble common bed and breakfasts and give tourists a much better view than is found in the city. The environmental consciousness of this people is evident in their use of organic and natural building processes. Coupling the cultural hotels with the castles from years' past, tourists will find the medieval cities to be of ancient glory yet quiet enough to concentrate on each piece of intrinsic beauty. When a tourist sees the stately maturity of a castle from the porch of their traditional-style bed and breakfast, they will recognize the great feat Romania has accomplished in maintaining their traditional heritage while allowing the country to modernize where necessary.

MOUNTAIN CLIMBING

Tourists should not confuse the mountain climbing of Romania with the feats of those who scale Mount Everest or other reputable mountains. The Carpathian Mountains found in Romania are more suited for those who desire a leisure hike to an awaiting plateau or cliff that holds the best views available in Romania. Tourists will be interested to know that in all Europe, the largest population of bears is found in the Carpathian Mountains. Tourists looking for desolate hikes and breathtaking views popping with color should plan to visit Romania during the fall months. Romania's seasons align with those of the United States, so the fall months of September to November provide the greatest array of colors and suitable hiking weather. The cities surrounding the Carpathian Mountains are almost as unique as the mountains themselves. Comprised of a people who refuse to abandon their former way of life, the residents of these cities are often accommodating to tourists, allowing them to watch them go about their ancient form of life. Many of these surrounding cities also have unique travel accommodations so that tourists can stay among those living a different way of life.

Festival Attendance

There is nothing more cultural in Romania than attending one of the many festivals that keep the Romanian calendar full of heritage. Today, Romania's festivals have become some of the most respected festivals of the day due to the ability to include both the heritage of the country with the modern inclination of the country as exhibited in its music and politics. The most popular area for these festivals is Transylvania, where the famous Transylvania International Film Festival is held every year. There are dozens of other festivals in Romania, some centered on music, food, and political demonstrations, while others are simply social gatherings with food. Tourists can find more information about the festivals officially sponsored by Romania at the following link: http://romaniatourism.com/festivals-events.html. Centering a trip on a specific festival is a tremendous way to relax while also seeing Romania's true culture.

Beaching

When tourists think of Romania, often the image of castles and year-round cold weather comes to mind. Such thoughts are simply not true and tourists will be pleased to know that there are some beautiful beaches fed from the waters of the Black Sea, leaving tourists with the ability to feed their desire for relaxation on a beach. A beautiful contrast, the Black Sea is bordered by beaches of golden sands, leaving tourists with beautiful sunsets and an aesthetic beach smoothed each night by the rising tide. Tourism on the local beaches has grown dramatically in the past ten years, taking the focus of much Romania's tourism industry. With vendors on every beach and travel packages that provide unlimited food and drink on the beach, tourists will find that Romania's beaches completely meet the desire for relaxation.

The Top-Rated Attractions of Romania

The following section will focus on tourist attractions in Romania that received the highest praise in recent years. While this list is not exhaustive, the goal of this chapter is to provide tourists with a greater sense of direction as they begin planning for their vacation to Romania.

The Old Town

One of the first settlements in the history of Bucharest, the Old Town is home to buildings built during the 15th and 16th centuries. The Old Town has a tremendous historical edge, giving tourists interested in unique locations the perfect destination. Thousands of years ago, the Old Town was considered the seat of the government, with princes and kings keeping their government offices in this area. With the center of government being in the Old Town, trade also became one of the primary foundations of the economy for this area. During the 1980s, a particularly divisive portion of Romania's history included its leader Nicolae Ceausescu razing part of the city so that he could remove some of the heritage for his new government. The city and Romania as a whole survived this attempt at creating a Socialist capital but the scars of this regime still exist in the Old Town. For most of the 1900s, the Old Town was regarded as a financially destitute area, low-income housing dominating the deteriorating infrastructure; however, the city's health and appeal become the focus of various humanitarian cases and the city gradually grew back and is now respected. Today, those efforts to revitalize the city have resulted in the Old Town becoming one of the most popular tourist destinations in Romania. Tourists will enjoy the combination of a cobblestone street that also has movie theaters, restaurants, and modern bookstores.

PALACE OF PARLIAMENT

Second only to the Pentagon, the Palace of Parliament is one of the world's largest administrative buildings and is the center of Romanian government. Today, the authoritative building demands the respect and admiration so many tourists bring to it every year. With a directory of more than 3,000 rooms that take up an astounding 330,000 square meters, this building is one of Romania's architectural crowns. During the tumultuous reign of Nicolae Ceausescu, the building also doubled as the living quarters and home of the feared leader. While the building is immaculate and the pride of many Romanians, its construction came at a cost. The destruction of parts of the Old Town was completed solely so that the expanse of the Palace of Parliament could be completed. So while the building is beautiful, many wished its establishment had not come at the cost of residences in the Old Town. During the thirteen-year tenure of the building's completion, more than 20,000 workers and 700 architects teamed together to complete the building. While much of Romania was starving in poverty, the Palace of Parliament was completed, casting an ominous face to the Ceausescu Regime that cared little for the health and prosperity of the citizens. During the Ceausescu Regime, citizens had to walk past the ornate structure each day reminded of the horrible inequality of life in the country. Today, the ornate building demonstrates the effects that socialism can have on a country, forever reminding Romanians of how far they've come.

While the building stands as a beautiful symbol of Romanian architecture, it is also a symbol of the slow growth of the government, many portions of the building remaining unfinished. Today, there are numerous museums located within the Palace of Parliament, the most notable being the famous National Museum of Contemporary Art. Another museum in the Palace of Parliament showcases the immense luxury that Ceausescu enjoyed prior to being overthrown in the subsequent coup d'état. The Palace of Parliament is more than a mere tourist attraction, it is a landmark. Tourists should visit this location during their vacation so that they can fully appreciate the hard work and resilience of the Romanian people.

ROMANIAN ATHENAEUM

Tourists to the Romanian Athenaeum will not merely be treated to one of the most ornate structures in Romania, they will also be treated to one of the best sounding orchestras in country with the Romanian George Enescu Philharmonic. Designed in the late 19th century, the Romanian Athenaeum was the caring endeavor of Albert Galleron, a French architect who had previously designed private houses within Bucharest. Later, Galleron designed the building that housed the National Bank of Romania near Galati. Galleron designed the building to resemble the architecture of Greek temples, six columns steadying the front end of the 41-meter dome that pierces the sky. While the outside of this building amazes tourists, the inside is where the true beauty is found. Inside, the ceilings of the building are painted gold and bear the resemblance of leaves. There are numerous balconies that allow tourists the privilege of overlooking the beautifully manicured lawns surrounding the building. Finally, the true focus of the residence is the auditorium that houses 652 attendees who are treated to the sweet sounds of the Romanian George Enescu Philharmonic Orchestra. Along the top of the inside of the building, a fresco that is 70 meters from end to end and over three meters tall tells the romantic, albeit tragic, history of Romania. Though the prime time to visit the Romanian Athenaeum is while one of the legendary concerts is taking place, there is enough history and plants along the garden that can be explored during the orchestra's off time. This tourist attraction will be of utmost interest to tourists who desire to compliment the luxury of their vacation with historical and artist flair.

STRAVROPOLEOS CHURCH

There is little doubt that one of Romania's primary tourist sectors is historical attractions. While the beaches will be discussed further in this section, Romania's history takes precedence over most beautiful attractions; therefore, it is no surprise that the churches of Romania draw almost as many tourists as the beaches of the Black Sea. One such church is the Stavropoleos Church, still used today and constructed by Ioanikie Startonikeas, a Greek monk. The intricacy of this church will leave tourists amazed that something this beautiful could be created with the rudimentary tools Startonikeas had. Standing tall with ornate rock spirals, the Stavropoleos Church remains the second-most visited attraction in the capital city of Bucharest. Inside, smooth wood adorns the walls and surrounds a beautiful courtyard that is host to hundreds of flowers. The wood icons on the inside of the church depict the historical beauty of the church and plenty of beautiful photo opportunities are found throughout the church. In the middle of the courtyard, tourists will find a graveyard with tombstones that are more 300 years old. At one time, the church was comprised of a hotel and monastery; however, they were destroyed in a fire shortly after the church's construction.

The church remains in good condition and tourists are able to explore most aspects of the courtyard and church. It has fallen prey to several earthquakes that used to plague the area; however, Bucharest has always repaired the church quickly, ensuring that it is available for tours during the peak summer tourism season. Tourists who are looking to see the religious culture of Romania from the beginning of the modern period will want to tour the church during their vacation.

OLD PRINCELY COURT AND CHURCH

Located in the Old City, the Old Princely Court was once the royal home of numerous admirable people such as the Wallachian princes of whom Vlad Tepes was the most famous. Vlad Tepes, known more notoriously as Vlad the Impaler, would one day be the subject for the novel written by Bram Stoker, *Dracula*. With such mystery surrounding the court, tourists will enjoy imagining the terrifying moments that would have taken place on this court thousands of years ago. Today, tourists are greeted by a stone statue of what an artist believed Vlad looked like, his eyes glancing over anyone who dare enter his former occupancy. The courtyard has fallen into serious disrepair, an understandable result of the years of tourists who have walked around its breadth. In the late 1500s, efforts were made by Mircea Ciobanul to restore the palace to a brighter and more positive image in the minds of the citizens. Additionally, Ciobanul also repaired numerous portions of the palace that Vlad had allowed to fall into disrepair. As Ciobanul attempted to restore the palace to its original beauty, skilled craftsman began flooding into the Old City, hoping for a chance to aid in the restoration of such a notable project. The effect of this sudden surge of talent to one area caused many of the surrounding houses and structures to be renovated to match the palace. Almost 100 years after the initial construction of the Palace, Ciobanul added another building adjacent to the palace: the Old Princely Court Church. After the completion of the church, the complex of buildings would be reserved for the coronation of Romanian kings for the following two centuries. Today, tourists can enjoy parading around the grounds, seeing numerous statutes and constructs that have survived years of disrepair. Of utmost interest, the Old Court Museum is located at the middle of the courtyard and contains artifacts that have been found during years of renovation around the grounds.

REVOLUTION SQUARE

Not all of Romania's tourist destinations lack present life and point to the previous life of Romanian dictators; some have found a unique way to combine both the past and the present and none is a greater or more enjoyable example than Revolution Square. Revolution Square adopted its name following the citizen's revolt against Nicolae Ceausecsu, a revolt that ended only after the hated dictator was removed from office. On that fateful night, the square hosted more than 100,000 furious Romanians who demanded the dictator's removal. The location was significant, since Nicolae had previously destroyed Romanian homes so he could build the square close enough to his Royal Palace so he could take long walks past the fountains with his family; however, the citizens grew angry at his frivolous use of their money and they refused to refer to the square as the Palace Square as Nicolae had demanded. Instead, they adopted the name Revolution Square and thus, the square was changed forever.

Tourists will want to be sure to check out the famous Monument of Rebirth, a statute with the names of 1,058 victims etched into its side. These victims were from the terrible revolution from which the square now bears its name. Additionally, a statue of Iuliu Maniu has been added to commemorate his allegiance to the Romanian people even after the Communist Party placed him in prison for his contradictory beliefs. Tourists will find the somber attitude of the square a stark reminder that while Romania has progressed as a modernized country, it still contains the tragic wounds of a country that was the victim of socialism and communism many years ago.

THE ARCH OF TRIUMPH

Not to be confused with the Arc de Triomphe from Paris, France, the Arch of Triumph is a monument in Bucharest Romania that closely resembles the French monument. Completed in 1922 and comprised solely of wood, the Arch of Triumph was originally a monument made to commemorate the lives of men who sacrificed their lives in the first World War. Its lifespan was short, however, and reconstruction efforts in 1936 led to the monument's destruction and replacement with a model completely made out of granite. The arch contains a great deal of Romanian culture and numerous Romanian architects and sculptors were requested to work on it. Sculptors such as Jalea and Dimitrie Paciurea were included in the construction efforts and tourists will recognize the Romanian flag that hands proudly between the arches. Today, the Romanian Army has designated this location as its primary military parade point, often marching under the arches en route to a parade location. In December, the arches become very important and daily celebrations commemorate the Romanian army. There are plenty of photo opportunities around the arches and tourists will enjoy the strong sense of nationalism that flows from the massive arch.

DIMITRIE GUSTI NATIONAL VILLAGE MUSEUM

Tourists interested in seeing Romanian culture from its first recorded days until its modern time period will want to visit the Dimitrie Gusti National Village Museum. In this museum, tourists will be led through more than 300 individual homes that exhibit the way of life Romanians experienced from the ancient times to the middle ages to the modern period. The museum has been in service since 1936 and homes are constantly being added or updated. Today, visitors are able to access the museum by means of the Herastrau Park. Of particular interest, the homes of this museum are all original: they were taken from all over Romania, disassembled, shipped by train to Bucharest, and then resembled to reveal a collection of homes that have survived the ages. The museum is not solely comprised of village homes, however; there are numerous artifacts also found within the homes, all artifacts original and found near the original site of the homes. Tourists will enjoy exploring the unique formations of the homes while also seeing the changes in design from century to century.

National Museum of Romanian History

Tourists anticipating their tour to Romania should remember that most of Romania's tourism industry hinges on Romania's historical sites. One site that encapsulates most historical experiences into one location is the National Museum of Romanian History. This museum is comprised of 60 rooms and is housed in a building fashioned in Neoclassic form and initially intended for Romania's postal department. The museum's exhibits are made from authentic or remanufactured artifacts, some dating as far back as the ancient villages of Romania. The historical data presented in this museum is thorough, giving tourists a glimpse at the history of Romania from the earliest records to the latest political offices. Within the museum, there are numerous exhibits but the one that towers over the rest is Trajan's Column, a replica of the monument built to commemorate the accomplishments of Trajan, the famous Roman emperor. The museum contains an abundance of gold items primarily from the era of the Dacian tribes. Additionally, the museum has the largest collection of jewels that previously belonged to Queen

Marie. The most expensive portion of the museum contains the Pietroasele Treasures, a collection of items coated in or completely comprised of gold. With these items dating to the fourth century, they were long atop the list of the most expensive treasure collections in the world; however, the discovery of the majestic jewels accompanying King Tutankhamen's pyramid slightly overshadowed the collection of Pietroasele Treasures. Tourists should plan on touring the museum for at least two days so that they can see everything it has to offer.

BUCHAREST PARKS

Romania is not just comprised of old, historical sites that showcase its culture; some of Romania's most popular attractions are found outside the city limits. One such place is the collection of Bucharest parks located around the outskirts of the city. Of these, the most noteworthy park is its oldest, the Cismigiu Park, which has a collection of lakes that tourists can navigate with rented rowboats. During the winter months, the park comes alive at night with ice skaters and lively music. The park has been open for more than 150 years, first allowing guests to enter its gates in 1860. The construction of the park was quite an undertaking, the majority of the foliage coming from trees imported from the Romanian mountains or Vienna.

A sister park to the Cismigiu Park, the Herastrau Park is on 400 acres and as mentioned earlier, is the home of the famous Dimitrie Gusti National Village Museum. The Herastrau Park also houses rowboats with which tourists can slowly meander around the lake. The homes surrounding the park were constructed in the 19th and 20th centuries and showcase Romania's upper class businessmen. Eduard Redent provided his contribution to Romania's parks in 1906 with the addition of the Carol Park. This park is largely regarded as the most beautiful park in the country and is home to the Tomb of the Unknown Soldier. The summer months at Carol Park come alive with the Arenele Romane, an amphitheater of sorts fashioned to look like the famous Roman amphitheaters.

Romania's parks offer a tourist the ability to hop from space to space, experiencing the quiet and nostalgic side of Romania. The grounds of Romania's primary parks are well-maintained, giving tourists the perfect spot for professional photos while in Romania.

MAMAIA BEACHES

Bordering the eastern side of Romania, the Mamaia resort beaches attract thousands of tourists each month, remaining a popular destination in and out of tourist season. Crushed by the relentless pounding of the Black Sea, the sand that surrounds the exterior of the

Black Sea is among the finest sands in the world. Each morning, tourists are greeted by a shy sun that slowly rises from the horizon, casting its first rays across the mirror-like reflection of the sea. After a day basking in the hot rays of the sun, tourists are privileged to see the sun fall as it completes its rotation across the sky, once again smearing its brilliant beams across the horizon and surface of the sea as it is sucked up by the horizon. While tourists will find the sunrise and sunset breathtaking, an equally beautiful site is the less frequent rising of the moon. A phenomenon that occurs with little routine, the moon will infrequently gift its viewers with a pristine show as it slowly assumes the void left by the escaping sun.

For those seeking history in the country, Mamaia is first tourist location in Romania to fully center on a beach. Founded in 1905, even a location as young as Mamaia has seen the horrors of the growing government of the country, yet it still showcases all of the beauty of the country today. Tourists looking to relax and experience the finest luxury that Romania has to offer will greatly enjoy the beaches of the Mamaia resort.

CARPATHIAN MOUNTAINS

The final destination showcased in this chapter on Romania's top-rated tourist attractions is arguably the most beautiful and desolate scenery found in Romania:

the ornate and stately Carpathian Mountains. Stretching for an astounding 900 kilometers, the Carpathian Mountains allow tourists to hike from the depths of a green and lush valley to the peaks of the mountains where they will be eye-level with the clouds. Tourists will enjoy being able to go rafting, cave exploring, horseback riding, or even mountain biking at various points throughout the Carpathian Mountains. Tourists wanting to see the Carpathian Mountains during their most beautiful moments should consider visiting Romania during the fall months, as the mountain side will explode in the color of dying leaves while also remaining dry enough to support weeklong hikes. Tourists will enjoy being able to camp outside or also use one of the few lodges that dot the mountainside.

In conclusion, the top-rated tourist attractions of Romania showcased in this section give tourists the security that their trip to Romania will show them both the natural and cultural attractions of Romania. Romania's tourism remains among the cheapest in the world, often the most expensive portion of the vacation being the travel arrangements to arrive in Romania. Tourists can rest assured that even the small country of Romania is more than capable to accommodate the millions of tourists that cross its borders every year.

The Food of Romania

It has been said that while the foundation of tourism is the attractions, the structure and walls of a successful vacation are formed by the accommodations, accommodations that include food. Tourists curious about Romania's food will be relieved to hear that Romania has some of the most filling and savory food in the world. The following section will outline some of the most popular foods in Romania.

Sarmale

Combining the most popular of Romanian ingredients, the Sarmale of Romania is little more than a delicious cabbage roll served as a comfort food throughout the country. The staple of most Romanian weddings, Sarmale is especially popular at restaurants around the holidays, specifically Christmas and New Years Day. The dish is comprised of minced meat such as pork or poultry, combined with a mixture of onions, rice, and sour cabbage leaves. This combination is then boiled in a tomato juice that includes a special ingredient: sauerkraut. This dish becomes even more popular during the fasting season of the Eastern Orthodox religion, the locals often taking the dish and replacing the meat with vegetable-based alternatives such as beans. This dish is often eaten with the compliment of sour cream and hot mamaliga. This dish is not very expensive and has survived the test of time in the country, remaining one of the most popular dishes.

MAMALIGA

Referenced as a compliment to saramele, mamaliga is a popular soup in Romania, often served with sour cream to smooth out the flavor. The dish is comprised of corn flour that has been boiled with salt. Additionally, some locals will add sunflower oil depending on the region they are from. Mamaliga is a very popular dish due to the nutrients packed into its tasty broth, giving Romanians nourishment during the harsh winters. In some regions, the locals will add other ingredients such as cheese to add protein to the meal. When combined with cheese, Romanians refer to the dish as "bulz." The most attractive element of mamaliga is that it is prepared differently in each region of Romania. Tourists will want to experience this dish in each location they tour.

MICI

A popular finger-food of Romania, Mici is famously referred to as "Small Ones." This dish is a popular staple of barbecues, parties, and street vendors due to its mobility and taste. Often, its scent will travel for hundreds of feet, allowing those desiring its taste to find it easily. To make this dish, Romanians take minced pork (a staple of Romanian meat production), combine it with beef, spices, garlic, and sodium bicarbonate before rolling the meat into a tight roll that is then grilled to seal the juices within the crusty exterior. The final product resembles small hand-made sausages that are easily dipped in sauces such as barbecue sauce or mustard. Additionally, some restaurants have begun serving the sausages between bread, resembling a hot dog but with more spice. Unless a tourist has dietary restrictions against meat, the mici will undoubtedly become one of their favorite meals while in Romania.

CIORBă DE BURTă

While ciorbă de burtă is not a dish for everyone, failing to include it in Romania's favorite dishes would leave this tour guide incomplete. The bold and spicy flavor of this soup will leave tourists breathing heavily; however, the taste is unmatched and many Romanians consider this the finest soup offered in county. Translated as Beef Tripe Soup, ciorbă de burtă is comprised of the soft meat found in the stomach of the cow, numerous variations of bones, vegetables, garlic, and topped with vinegar. Some restaurants will even top the dish with red hot peppers, adding a bold flavor to the symphony of spices that protrude from the soup's smooth broth. While some tourists might be scared away from the odd ingredients, there is little doubt that a vacation to Romania is not complete without at least attempting this bold dish.

Pomana Porcului

True Romanian delicacy includes the cultural ingredients of meat and strong spices and Pomana Porcului is no exception. This dish, which translated literally means "Honoring the Pig," is among the oldest dishes in the country. Additionally, the dish is the focal point of a tradition in which a pig is slaughtered outside in the month of December. After slaughtering the pig, the meat from the pig is placed in a pan that is padded with fat from the pig. This meat is then left to crisp in the pan, leaving a delicious meat that is often coupled with pickles. This dish is often served around the Christmas holiday, many restaurants advertising that they have the resources to serve fresh Pomana Porcului. Tourists should be warned, however; some restaurants will attempt to cook this dish using refrigerated pork. The taste is markedly different and there is no replacement for the meat from a freshly slaughtered pig.

Jumări

In conjunction with the previous dish, Jumări is made from taking the bacon from the freshly slaughtered pig and frying it in the grease that previously fried the pomana porcului. The resulting dish, a crunchy and greasy bowl of bits of bacon, is the perfect appetizer for the Christmas feast. To complete the appetizer, locals will often retain the heat of the meat, serving the dish quite warm and topped with slices of raw onions. The final element of a complete serving of jumări is a shot of plum brandy that is available at any local grocery store.

COZONAC

The Eastern Orthodox religion does not manifest itself only in the holidays or churches of the country; indeed, the religion has even found its way to the cuisine of the country, dictating not only eating habits but also certain dishes. One such dish is cozonac, a sweet bread that is traditionally eaten around Christmas or Easter. The sweet bread is a staple Romanian dessert around these holidays and demonstrates the culture of Romanian cuisine. From the outside, this sweetbread hardly looks different than a loaf of ordinary wheat bread; however, upon opening the loaf, tourists are exposed to the true beauty of this bread. The interior of this dish is comprised of walnut paste, poppy seed paste, and numerous raisins or Turkish delights. These interior ingredients are combined and spread in a circular pattern within the bread, a process that requires the person making the bread to kneed the bread in a particular fashion. The result is bread that leaves tourists with a wholesome yet sweet flavor on their tongues. Tourists are able to find this bread in Romanian grocery stores year-round; however, the homemade ones, only available during one of the religious seasons, are markedly better in taste and leave the consumer with a standard for Romanian culture.

Drob de miel

Loosely translated, the name for this dish means "Lamb Drob" and truly, that is what the dish resembles. Looking similar to a meatloaf, drob de miel is a dish that has a foundation of lamb meat that has been stuffed with boiled eggs, green onions, milk, and herbs that can include parsley, garlic, or dill but depend on the region. There are several variations of drob de miel but the most popular variation serves the meal cold. Serving such a dense meat cold has caused some tourists to refrain from partaking in it; however, the combination of cold lamb meat and eggs makes the dish seem almost like a breakfast casserole.

Papanaśi

There is hardly a dish that is regarded as a more popular dessert than Papanaśi. This dish, which finds its roots in the northern cuisine of Romania, is nothing more than a clump of cottage cheese that has been shaped as a doughnut and topped with sour cream and a jam that depends on the region of origin. Tourists are encouraged to try the papanaśi that is covered in blueberry jam. This dish is consistently ranked the highest-favored tourist dessert in the country and will undoubtedly become the favorite of any new tourist.

Salata de Boeuf

The dish, salata de boeuf, is a beef salad that combines diced vegetables fresh from the gardens of the restaurant and meat. The meat and vegetables are closely diced, making the dish a delicacy in Romania. Because of the ease with which restaurants can make salata de boeuf, tourists will find that this dish is among the most economical choices for lunch or supper. While the initial dishes of salata de boeuf used beef as the only meat, certain regions of Romania have chosen to give patrons the choice of either beef or chicken. Tourists will find this dish to be similar to a salad that has been combined with a sandwich.

Ciorba Radautean

Another soup that is popular with most Romanians is the ciorba radautean. This traditional soup is another example of the regional differences that can transform a single dish. This dish is one of the latest to make it to the Romanian food scene, arriving in the late 1970s. Originally, this soup was made by smaller restaurants that hosted tourists and other locals who were too poor for the expensive tripe soup of the country. Additionally, some locals had complained that the tripe soup was too heavy on ingredients and left them tired after consumption. After the introduction of ciorba radautean, the locals were able to achieve the same level of taste while substituting chicken instead of the more expensive beef. The soup is comprised of sour cream, garlic, vinegar, and other herbs. Tourists will find this soup the perfect complement to a meal serving a main meal that consists of a meat-based dish.

The food of Romania is exquisitely cultural. Some tourists will find the food delicious while others will be more hesitant. Tourists who are concerned about the taste of the food should not worry since there are national restaurants available for attendance in Romania. Tourists should rest assured that whether or not they dine on the finest Romanian cuisine, they will remain fed!

Touring in Romania

Once in Romania, touring the country is an effortless job that simply requires a tourist to use common sense and plan his trip well in advance. Prior to getting to Romania, however, tourists should familiarize themselves with the travel rules. To enter Romania by flight, tourists will need to have a valid passport if they are traveling from somewhere outside of the European Union. Citizens from an EU country do not need a passport, a mere national identity card is sufficient enough to warrant entry. For tourists required to use a passport to enter the country, they will be issued a travel visa once they arrive at their airport. While these two travel arrangements will cover most citizens, tourists from Africa, Asia, or the Middle East should consult the list of countries that have bene posted to the Foreign Affairs Ministry list. Countries on this list require more identification and a pre-approved visa letter before they will be allowed entrance into Romania. As always, tourists can check the following website to see if they need a visa or a pre-approved visa letter: https://www.mae.ro/en/node/2040.

Once the tourist has secured passage through customs in the airport, they should consider exchanging their money for the official Romanian currency, the Leu.

The Leu supports denominations from 1 all the way to 500 and is made from a high-grade plastic, making the currency as close to indestructible as current currencies have found. Breaking the leu into smaller denominations, the Bani is Romania's currency of coin, splitting one leu into .50, .10, and even smaller denominations that would be equal to the penny from the United States. Tourists should be warned that using the Euro as a means of payment for a cash transaction is not accepted in Romania. This often confuses tourists since most of the cash prices are presented in Euro denominations. This often works for Romanian citizens since they are familiar with the exchange rates of the European Union. Because tourists will not be as familiar with the exchange rates, they should exchange all of their money to Romanian currency at an exchange bureau and then exchange their Romanian currency back to the currency of their country on their return flight home. While the airport offers currency exchange services, tourists should refrain from using these services since the airports will often post an incorrect exchange rate that will skim the top of the tourists' currency as a "service fee." The exchange bureaus located around Romania are more fair and will often perform the currency exchange for free. Currently, one Euro averages an exchange rate of four or five Lei while one dollar from the United States is equal to over 4 lei. To get a better perspective as to how much money a

Another element of the financial customs of Romania involves tipping. In Romania, tipping is considered a requirement at the end of every meal or service, regardless of the level or amount of service imparted. While the size of the tip can vary depending on the formality and level of service, tips are accepted. Tourists should also recognize that restaurants will often exclude the service fees from their menu, causing the final price of the food to reflect a 5% increase after the bill has been delivered to the customer. The average tip for a restaurant is 10% and customers' discretion can increase that tip from 15-20% depending on the level of service. Tourists are encouraged to tip after cosmetic and taxi services as well, though this tip can be markedly lower and averages 5% of the total cost. Additionally, tourists should consider tipping their tour guide after a guided tour as well. Some tour guides will not desire a tip but if one person offers to tip and the tip is accepted, all members of the party should tip.

Shopping has become a favorite of most tourists and Bucharest is the shopping capital of the country. The most popular malls in Bucharest are the AFI Palace, Baneasa Shopping City, Promenada Mall, or ParkLake. These malls all offer a great selection of both domestic styles as well as styles from around the world. Tourists should refrain from relying on street vendors for their goods while in Romania. Most street vendors will only sell goods, albeit at a fair price, but will grossly overprice their souvenirs. Romanian clothing has become world famous for its value and affordable cost. Leather goods and textiles are becoming more popular as tourists bring goods back to their home countries and introduce Romanian fashion around the world. Tourists should consider purchasing a new pair of Romanian dress shoes or a dress while in Romania; however, they must remember that all goods purchased in Romania will have to be claimed at customs so purchasing a large amount of clothing might cause unnecessary trouble when re-entering their country.

After arriving in Romania, tourists will have to secure transportation. This is the primary area of tourist complaints while in Romania. Romania's infrastructure greatly reflects the culture and heritage of the country and getting around in Romania can be very frustrating. Romania has a lack of highways and those that do exist are mostly one-way, causing short distances to take a long time to cross. The speed limit around the country is primarily 55 miles per hour and the high traffic on the limited roads can reduce this average to a mere 35 miles per hour for most roads. The cheapest form of travel in the country is the railroads that stretch across the entire country. Most cities have a train station, but these train stations are also prone to terrible reliability and a day can be ruined by an inoperable train. The best option for touring at a reasonable cost that is also reliable would be taxi or bus service. The taxi drivers are adept at driving the one-way highways and can often get tourists to their destination in the shortest time possible despite the line of traffic stretching between cities. The other great option, bus, is both reliable and even more low-priced than most taxi services. The benefit of using a bus service is that the many scams that plague the taxi industry are not found and the buses usually charge a low-price flat rate for all patrons. Longer travel arrangements that are near 150 miles should be traveled using the coach options. Traveling by coach will afford the tourist the most comfortable option with minimal inconvenience and cost. For trips that are longer than 150 miles, tourists should consider using one of the domestic flight services. Flying in Romania can be more of a hassle but is low-priced enough that tourists will find the hassle more than worth its affordability.

Another element to touring Romania that must be addressed is travel insurance. Romania is one of the most secure and safe countries to tour, but tourists should avoid the risk of paying for a hospital visit while in Romania. The availability of travel insurance adds a level of protection to a tourist's vacation that relieves a great amount of stress. While travel insurance covers hospital visits while in the country, it also covers the theft of goods. Romania is not known for scams surrounding its tourism industry; however, tourists will sometimes find themselves caught up in a petty crime that results in the hassle of shopping for new items to replace the ones recently stolen, all while reducing their travel budget. For this reason, tourists are strongly encouraged to take out at least a small travel insurance policy. Often, if no claims are made, some of this money can be recouped following the vacation. Tourists should not fear the inconvenience of a hospital visit or a theft while in Romania but should remain prepared should such an event occur.

The climate of Romania largely resembles the United States, with four seasons that correlate with the current seasons of the United States. While the peak tourist season in the country is during the summer months, many tourists assert that the best time of year to tour Romania is during the fall months when the Carpathian Mountains explode in different shades of orange, red, and brown. Additionally, the lack of tourists during this time of year gives tourists more time to enjoy the various attractions. Because most of Romania's tourism hinges on the natural attractions and churches, tourists will enjoy the balmy cool days of Romania's fall months coupled with the gorgeous sunsets for which Romania is famous. Regardless of the time of year, tourists should remain confident that their time in Romania will be enjoyable and beautiful.

With Romania in the European Union, many tourists often wonder what to expect regarding electricity and network connectivity. Tourists will want to pack an adaptor if their items requiring electoral connection use a three prong that requires the standard socket found in the United States or United Kingdom. The electrical sockets found in Romania use a three printed pin with an electrical connection that varies between 210-230 volts. With a simple adaptor, tourists can enjoy a consistent electrical connection that will meet their needs. For tourists concerned that the internet connection of the country is sub-par, they will be relieved to find that the internet of Romania is among the fastest internet connections in the world. Romania ranks 6th globally in the race for fastest internet. Most public locations offer free public wifi and the average cafe will have high-speed internet available for free or with the purchase of a drink. The mobile network coverage of Romania is average but not with the same speeds enjoyed in the United States or United Kingdom. Nationwide, the country enjoys mobile internet connection speeds that vary between 3G and 4G. For tourists trying to communicate with those back home, the country code for Romania's phone lines is +40.

Historically, Romania has been a healthy country, with no current parasite or health issues being reported. For tourists needing emergency medical attention, any public calling phone or their cellphone will connect them with medical services when 112 is dialed. Tourists who rush to a hospital for medical attention will often be accommodated quickly through the state-owned hospitals and medical facilities. Tourists needing an English-speaking doctor are encouraged to seek young doctors as more of them know English than the older doctors. Tourists are encouraged to bring an adequate supply of prescription medicines with them since it is difficult to receive prescription medicine in Romania without a doctor's note. For needs that require over-the-counter medicine, most Romanian pharmacies carry the appropriate medicines at an affordable cost.

Touring Romania is practically effortless and the famous Romanian hospitality will keep tourists cared for when they most need it. Tourists should take the necessary precautions against dangers while in Romania but should be rest assured that Romania is among the safest countries to tour.

The Unique Hotels of Romania

Not only does the food of Romania pose a unique experience for tourists, so can staying in a hotel overnight! Romania is home to some of the most unique hotels in the world, all showcasing either the culture, heritage, or climate of their location in a memorable way. The following section will focus on some of the most unique overnight accommodations that tourists can take advantage of while in Romania.

The Ice Hotel

Perhaps the most unique and cultural living accommodation in Romania, the Ice Hotel is located 6,700 feet above sea level and is only accessible by cable-car from the nearby city of Balea Cascada. Located in the Carpathian Mountains and between the various peaks of the Fagaras Massif, there is hardly a more suitable overnight accommodation for tourists exploring the beauty of the Carpathian Mountains. This hotel, Romania's newest, is rebuilt every year so that the four-foot long ice bricks harvested from Balea Lake do not become weak with the changing climate. Every time the hotel is rebuilt, a new design is created so that the hotel is never the same for returning tourists. In 2012, the ice hotel boasted of 12 rooms, a bar, an ice-lounge, and a restaurant that served cultural dishes. As the years have progressed and the hotel has gained popularity, other accommodations have been added nearby to mimic the ice hotel's unique look. One year after the hotel's inception, an Ice Church was added nearby so that tourists could be baptized in the cold and white interior of the Eastern Orthodox church. As the church has increased its line of services offered, it has recently begun offering weddings in the church as well. While tourists will likely not use any of these services, the unique nature of the hotel demands at least a visit from the outside, true experience-seekers requiring an overnight stay to truly appreciate the work that went into building each year's design. For tourists concerned that the hotel is a difficult experience, tourists have raved about the soft mattresses placed on the beds made of ice. The bed sheets are thermal and the blankets are often covered in soft furs. Additionally, for the convenience of tourists, every tourist is given a sleeping bag to ensure they remain warm. The current rates at the hotel are $89 a night, a nominal fee considering the experience. Tourists interested in booking a night at the famous Ice Hotel should check out the hotel's website: http://hotelofice.ro/. This experience will leave tourists wanting to return every year, joining the thousands of repeat tourists the Ice Hotel sees every year.

Hotel Residence Arc de Triomphe

Nestled near the country's most notable landmark, the Hotel Residence Arc de Triomphe provides tourists with the most reasonable means of experiencing Romania's hub of civilization. The hotel is recognized by the National Register of Historic Places in Romania, giving the hotel the credence many tourists demand in luxury overnight accommodations. Each room in this historic hotel is made with luxury in mind, glistening baths, mini-bars, ornate desks and bed frames, and international telephones just to name a few of the accommodations. The hotel offers free private parking, an upscale restaurant, airport shuttling, a dry cleaning and laundry service, and complimentary wireless internet. Tourists interested in booking a night's stay at this historic residence are encouraged to check out the hotel's website at: www.residencehotels.com.ro. With the Arc de Triomphe in clear sight, this hotel truly offers one of the best views offered in the country.

Grand Hotel Continental

While Romania's natural attractions showcase the rugged beauty of the country, there is a contingent of Romania's beauty that is refined luxury and the Grand

Hotel Continental is great venue for tourists desiring luxury overnight accommodations. With 59 recently renovated rooms that maintain the hotel's cutting edge beauty, this location also houses six apartments for tourists or guests with extended stays in the country. Tourists have two elegant restaurants at their disposal: the Concerto and the Balkan Bistro. Additionally, the Victoria Club is a bar that exudes the elegance of the residence, boasting of mahogany furniture and leather sofas. Tourists are further indulged in their pursuit of elegance with the Eden Spa, a massage parlor that also offers beauty treatments. Each room has its own personal internet connection, giving tourists first-hand access to a fast internet connection. Additionally, each room has an international phone, individual shower and bathtub, satellite television, mini-bar, and a safe deposit box. The hotel is located strategically close to the Royal Palace, the National Art Museum, and the Roman Athenaeum, giving tourists the perfect destination within walking distance of some of Romania's most famous attractions. Tourists interested in more information about this hotel can find information on the hotel's website: www.grandhotelcontinental.ro.

Hotel Camino Home

For tourists visiting the Old Town, they will find the Hotel Camino Home to be of utmost attraction and elegance. Built in the late 1800s, this hotel operates as a bed and breakfast. Only recently has the residence been renovated and repurposed as a bed and breakfast. With history seeping from the halls and floors, tourists are treated to luxury that includes Romanian culture. Within this residence, the choice room is one that offers a balcony giving tourists the prime view of the three major cathedrals located in Cluj. Each room has a mini-bar, kitchenette, wireless internet, and the ability to house pets. Operating as a bed and breakfast, tourists will appreciate the autonomy this residence offers. Many tourists have remarked about the residence's ability to give tourists the feeling they are in their own home. While the amenities and view of this residence are extravagant and reason enough for tourists to enjoy this hotel, the remarkably low price of each night's stay makes it the top overnight attraction in Cluj. For only $55 a night, each room is rented to tourists. Additionally, this price includes the taxes and breakfast. Tourists will enjoy the availability of nearby attractions including the Unirii Square, the Cluj National Opera, and the Museum Square, the metropolis of Cluj's nightlife. Tourists desiring the comfort their residence back home offers them will appreciate the Hotel Camino Home.

VISCRI 125

For tourists desiring an overnight residence that has remained in the 18th century despite the current period, the Viscri 125 has retained the culture of the day the hotel was made. Constructed in the mid-1700s and then renovated in 2011 to improve the living conditions while retaining the 1700s look, this residence remains a luxurious overnight accommodation despite keeping the culture of the Saxon life it once supported. Nearby, a church that was made in the 14th century remains in operation and is toured daily by tourists looking at the strict adherence to the Eastern Orthodox religion that most of Romania practices. This church has recently been named a UNESCO World Heritage Site, placing it on the list of attractions every tourist to Romania should see. Viscri 125 is a collection of homes built during the days of the Saxon's inhabitation of Romania. These homes are located in the countryside of Romania, allowing them to remain out of the surge of modern practices that flood cities like Bucharest. Each room within this hotel holds a queen bed and hand-woven carpets adorn the floor. While the home lacks the luxurious amenities of other hotels in Romania, it does offer free wireless internet and a large open area where tourists can order food or simply sit and chat. The rate for a one-night stay in this residence is currently $65 and includes access to the complimentary buffet offered each morning for breakfast.

Tourists to this area of Romania are afforded more autonomy than most tourists and activities such as trekking, hiking, mountain climbing, hunting and hay stacking will keep the tourists busy outdoors. Tourists are also able to attend a variety of workshops sponsored at Viscri 125. These workshops center on how Saxons lived life so many years ago. Tourists interested in more information about Viscri 125 should check out their website at: www.viscri125.ro.

ARENA REGIA HOTEL AND SPA

Located in the heart of Romanian tourism, the Arena Regia Hotel and Spa gives tourists the perfect week-long accommodations for their vacation in Mamaia, the beach capital of Romania. This hotel resembles the typical beach-side resort, complete with gourmet restaurants and a gym. The hotel is one of the many overnight accommodations offered by the Marina Regia Residence that attracts the most tourists in the Black Sea area. For tourists who desire the autonomy of having their own home while on vacation, the residence also has 46 villas that run adjacent to the hotel. Open since 2011, the Arena Regia Hotel and Spa offers its tourists the ability to enjoy rooms with custom furniture, silk sheets, balconies from every room, international telephones, a mini-bar, and even more. In the general living space of the hotel, the Arena and Romeo and Juliet are two restaurants that leave tourists wanting to come back to the resort. For adults, the on-campus bar, the Colonial Club Restaurant and Bar, keeps its guests entertained until the early mornings. After the sun has set and the beach empties, tourists are encouraged to join the rest of the tenants in the in-door swimming complex for family fun. Perhaps the greatest attraction of this residence is its ability to host families at a low cost. Tourists using the Arena Regia Hotel and Spa will enjoy the nearby Danube Delta, Tomis and Histria in addition to the Murfalar Winery. Tourists desiring more information or a booking at the Arena Regia Hotel and Spa should check out their website at: www.marinaregia.com.

GRAND HOTEL TRAIAN

Tourists to the city of Iasi will want to consider staying at the famous Grand Hotel Traian, a hotel that has seen the majority of Romania's modern history. Built in 1882, this residence affords its customer the ability to get an up-close look at neo-classical Romanian architecture. Located in Eastern Romania's largest city, the Grand Hotel Traian is the pride and joy of the city, often compared with the Eiffel Tower of Paris since they were constructed around the same time. In addition to being one of the country's primary sources of luxury, it also holds historical notoriety as being the temporary residence and headquarters of the Romanian government at the end of World War II. It has housed some of Romania's most-loved celebrities, including Greta Garbo. The 68 rooms of this hotel are all adorned with antiques that the hotel has accumulated during its nearly 140-year tenure. Within the hotel, its two restaurants, Clasic and Salanul Alb, give its residents a taste of authentic Romanian culture while also offering global cuisine. Evening activities at the hotel include patronage of the London Pub, a bar that is elegant enough to demand a quiet atmosphere in stark contrast to the rowdy nightlife taking place outside of the hotel. This residence has recently become the favorite location of Romanian businesses since its three meeting rooms can each house more than 450 guests for daytime meetings. One element that distinguishes this hotel from other Romanian hotels is its available smoking rooms. The hotel offers all guests services such as parking, laundry and dry cleaning, room service, and room service. Tourists to the Grand Hotel Traian will enjoy the nearby attractions such as the Three Hierarchs Church, the Union Museum, and the Golia Monastery. Tourists interested in more information on the hotel are encouraged to check out the hotel's website: www.GrandHotelTraian.ro.

HOTEL CASA ROZELOR

Tourists spending their vacation in historic Brasov Romania should consider the affordable accommodations of the Hotel Casa Rozelor. This hotel, originally built in the 1400s, is officially recognized within the National Register of Historic Buildings. While accommodations in the hotel are beautiful, its lack of rooms makes it a hard residence in which to secure lodging. Often, tourists report they have to book the residence almost a year in advance. The hotel's brick architecture casts a cold yet historical aura over the building. Each room is tastefully decorated with antique furniture that has been collected by the museum since its inception. Each room is equipped with a television, complimentary wireless internet, a kitchen, and a private bathroom. Despite these limited accommodations, the hotel remains in constant demand and therefore, has a steep price tag that accompanies each night of stay. For one night, hotel room costs $85 and includes breakfast served in the main dining room. While the residence might be among the more expensive accommodations in the country, its proximity to some of the least expensive attractions in Romania makes it well worth the daily rate. Nearby, tourists will find the Black Church, a local history museum, Dracula's Castle, and the Rasnov Fortress. Tourists interested in more information on the residence or possibly booking a room can find more details on the hotel's website: www.casarozelor.ro.

Safari Danube Delta-Enisala Village

The Danube Delta has become one of Romania's most popular natural attractions and is now third on the list of most biologically diverse areas globally. Built in 1995 by an unnamed local architecture, the Safari Danube Delta is a collection of two cottages that allow tourists full autonomy is an isolated portion of Romania. With the nearest airport more than 180 miles away in Bucharest and the nearest city almost a half hour away in Tulcea, this isolated retreat center is a place tourists will find to be of utmost relaxation. Each cottage offers eight rooms and two suites. While the isolated nature of these hotel rooms takes away the amenities offered by a larger city, each room remains fully functional with wireless internet and air conditioning. From each window, the nearby lakes of Babadag and Razim Lakes are visible. Additionally, tourists can travel to the nearby Enisala Fortress for a glimpse of what life was like during the middle ages. The rates of the hotel rooms are very reasonably priced at $69 a night and include breakfast, lunch, and dinner. Tourists using the Safari Danube Delta are largely independent of tour groups and will find nearby activities such as bird watching, nature-walks, hiking, fishing, and boating at their disposal. For tourists who desire the safety of a larger tour group, daily archeology tours are offered. Tourists interested in more information on the Safari Danube Delta should consult the hotel's website: <u>safari.ro</u>.

KALNOKY MANOR

Following the format of most Romanian hotels, the Kalnoky Manor is comprised of four cottages that combine to house ten rooms, each built well before the middle of the 1800s. The cottages have retained the culture of their origin, sporting large oak beams and plaster walls. The staff of the Kalnoky Major dresses in the historical garb of the former tenants and maintains life on the manor as it would have transpired over two hundred years ago. This hotel has achieved notoriety as being the first heritage hotel the country recognized. While each room operates with electricity, this is the extent of the technology of the residence. No televisions or wireless internet is available at this location due to the staff's attempt to retain the culture of the site. Tourists interested in booking a room should consult the hotel's website at <u>www.transylvaniancastle.com</u>.

Indicated by the hotels featured above, many of Romania's hotels are simple cottages that have been divided into multiple rooms, allowing tourists to remain secure and comfortable in the residence while also seeing the historical aspect of Romania. While most of Romania's hotels are intended for couples or individuals, families will find better accommodations near the resorts of Mamaia. Tourists can be rest assured that the living accommodations of Romania are among the nicest in the world.

Communicating and Staying Safe in Romania

Of the few frustrations tourists will face during their vacation in Romania, communicating will be chief. This frustration seems to be nearing an end, however, with the rise of Romanians speaking English. Today, the majority of young Romanians speak English, meaning that tourists should have little trouble communicating with a young Romanian. The trouble comes with someone is tasked with speaking to an older Romanian or one who does not speak English. Romanian is a hard language to master and most tourists will be unable to learn a large collection of phrases they can use to communicate throughout the country. While speaking in Romanian may be a daunting task, the list below is a collection of phrases that tourists will use the most while in Romania.

"Da" ~ "Da" is translated to mean "Yes" and is usually accompanied by one nodding his head.

"Nu" ~ "Nu" is the contradiction to "Da," translated as "No" and is accompanied by   either shaking the index finger back and forth or shaking one's head side to side.

"Tu" ~ "Tu" is the informal word that refers to someone a tourist would be talking with. Loosely translated, it means "you."

"Dumneavoastră"~ "Dumneavoastră" is the more formal version of "you" that is often used to denote polite address for a superior. For instance, one would use this word when addressing a person who is much older; however, after using this phrase once, it is often acceptable to refer to the respected person as "tu" for the remainder of the conversation.

"Mulțumesc" ~ "Mulțumesc" is the polite way to say "thank you" in Romanian. Following the culture, this phrase is often accompanied by a hand shake or a kiss. While this is the formal version of "thank you," many Romanians simply use the phrase "merci" when accepting a gift.

"Cu plăcere~ "Cu plăcere" is the Romanian phrase for "with pleasure." This phrase is often repeated after a person says "thank you." Most Romanians do not following the American culture of greeting by saying "you're welcome" after one states "thank you."

"Nu, mulțumesc" ~ "Nu, mulțumesc" is the polite way to say "no thank you" and turn down an offer. While there are different phrases that also mean this, most Romanians simply use this for all instances of turning

someone down because it is the fastest way of politely rejecting one's offer.

"Te rog" ~ "Te rog" is the polite way of saying "please" in Romanian. Its similar phrase "vă rog" is sometimes used as well but the more polite version is "te rog."

"Scuză-mă" ~ "Scuză-mă" is the polite way of saying "excuse me" in Romanian. This phrase is acceptable both as a question to be repeated in addition to asking to move past someone.

"Salut" ~ "Salut" is the polite phrase meaning "hello." It is considered informal but is acceptable when addressing friends or family.

These phrases will allow tourists to communicate politely with Romanians but will do little to allow direct communication. For this reason, tourists are encouraged to use the aid of a tour guide when traveling. While the communication barrier is one of the hindrances to Romanian tourism, there are also some safety concerns that should be addressed before concluding this tour guide.

Romania's infrastructure is well behind the times, meaning that its road system is falling apart. Because the threat of becoming stranded due to a flat tire is inevitable in Romania, tourists should take care to never travel alone. Additionally, tourists must remain cautious when driving around a horse and buggy. Many times, the buggy driver will swerve to avoid a pot hole, sometimes placing his buggy directly into the oncoming traffic. Motorists are expected to give right-of-way to the horse and buggy and should pull over if this happens. Tourists should also watch out for the stray dogs that have become commonplace in Romania. While most of these dogs are harmless, some contain terrible diseases and are not afraid to bite someone if incited. Tourists should be cautious if entering the country via road as well. The border agents often rifle through personal belongs under the ruse of looking for contraband. While doing this, it is not uncommon for border agents to take personal belongings if no one is looking. Tourists are welcome to watch the border agents search their vehicle, a precaution that usually discourages theft.

Tourists need not worry about being physically assaulted any more than they would in their own country. Historically, Romania has been a very secure country; however, some people, when discouraged by their poverty, will prey on the innocent tourists. Tourists should always have the phone number for their country's embassy handy in case of large theft or kidnapping. While these crimes are very rare and likely the embassy will never be called, it is a necessary precaution to take while touring Romania.

In conclusion, Romania is a country of rare, natural beauty. A devoutly religious country, Romania is home to hundreds of churches, giving tourists a virtually uncapped selection of sites to tour during their vacation. Tourists should take time to enjoy the different locations, culture, and people. Though Romania's economy is not among the world's leaders, it is sufficient and the people of Romania are a happy people. Tourists can be sure that the people of Romania will make sure they have a wonderful visit.

REFERENCES

"10 Travel Tips for First Time Visitors in Romania [2020 Guide]." *Romanian Friend,* www.romanianfriend.com/blog/first-time-visitor.

"12 Top-Rated Attractions & Things to Do in Bucharest: PlanetWare." *PlanetWare.com,* www.planetware.com/romania/top-rated-attractions-things-to-do-in-bucharest-rom-1-2.htm.

"14 Mouth-Watering Romanian Foods That Everyone Should Try." *Romanian Food | 14 Traditional Dishes That Will Warm Your Soul,* rolandia.eu/en/blog/romanian-culture-traditions/14-mouth-watering-romanian-foods-that-everyone-should-try.

Andre, et al. "8 Most Beautiful Cities in Romania." *Travel Away,* 29 Aug. 2017, travelaway.me/most-beautiful-cities-romania/.

"Arc De Triomphe Paris." *A Top Tourist Spot In the City of Lights,* arcdetriompheparis.com/.

"Arena Regia Hotel & Spa." *Romania,* romaniatourism.com/hotels/hotel-arena-regia.html.

Condrea, Diana. "The Carpathian Mountains: The
        Wildest Side of Europe." *Uncover Romania*, 8
        Feb. 2020, www.uncover-
        romania.com/attractions/nature/carpathian-
        mountains/.

Dunford, Jane. "10 Of the Best Things to Do in Cluj-
        Napoca, Romania: a Local's Guide." *The
        Guardian*, Guardian News and Media, 27 Jan.
        2020,
        www.theguardian.com/travel/2020/jan/27/cluj
        -napoca-romania-city-break-locals-guide.

Gheorghe, Georgeta. "12 Romanian Phrases You Need to
        Know." *Culture Trip*, The Culture Trip, 29 Sept.
        2017,
        theculturetrip.com/europe/romania/articles/12
        -romanian-phrases-you-need-to-know/.

"Grand Hotel Continental, Bucharest." *Romania*,
        romaniatourism.com/hotels/hotel-grand-
        continental-bucharest.html.

"Grand Hotel Traian." *Romania*,
        romaniatourism.com/hotels/hotel-grand-
        traian.html.

"Hotel Camino Home - Cluj Napoca." *Romania*,
        romaniatourism.com/hotels/hotel-camino-
        home-cluj-napoca.html.

"Hotel Casa Rozelor." *Romania*,
        romaniatourism.com/hotels/hotel-casa-
        rozelor.html.

"Hotel of Ice." *The Hotel of Ice, Romania's Ice Hotel near Balea Lake (Fagaras Mountains).* , romaniatourism.com/hotels/hotel-ice-romania.html.

"Hotel Residence Arc De Triomphe." *Romania,* romaniatourism.com/hotels/hotel-residence-arc-de-triomphe.html.

"Jewish Cemetery: Iaşi, Romania Attractions." *Lonely Planet,* 20 Sept. 2019, www.lonelyplanet.com/romania/moldavia/iasi/attractions/jewish-cemetery/a/poi-sig/1289180/360392.

"Kalnoky Manor." *Romania,* romaniatourism.com/hotels/hotel-kalnoky-manor.html.

Lonely Planet, www.lonelyplanet.com/romania/bucharest.

Lonely Planet, www.lonelyplanet.com/romania/moldavia/iasi.

Partner, Daniel GheorghitaManaging. "Top 10 Tourist Attractions in Romania." *Covinnus Travel. Tours of Romania and Eastern Europe,* 22 Dec. 2017, covinnus.com/top-10-tourist-attractions-romania/.

Serban, Adina, and Adina SerbanAdina. "Top 10 Romanian Foods - Most Popular Dishes in

Romania." *Chef's Pencil*, 21 Dec. 2019,
     chefspencil.com/top-10-romanian-foods/.

Sills-Dellegrazie, Jackie, et al. "12 Terrific Things to Do
     in Brasov Romania." *The Globetrotting
     Teacher*, 20 Jan. 2020,
     www.theglobetrottingteacher.com/things-to-
     do-in-brasov-romania/.

Sills-Dellegrazie, Jackie, et al. "15 Splendid Things to Do
     in Sibiu Romania." *The Globetrotting Teacher*,
     20 Jan. 2020,
     www.theglobetrottingteacher.com/things-to-
     do-in-sibiu-romania/.

Varga, Cory. "Guide to Mamaia, Romania." *You Could
     Travel*, You Could Travel, 3 Sept. 2019,
     www.youcouldtravel.com/travel-blog/guide-to-
     mamaia-romania.

Virtual Tourist See recent posts by Virtual Tourist. "Tips
     on Romania Warnings or Dangers - Stay Safe!"
     SmarterTravel, SmarterTravel, 16 Feb. 2017,
     www.smartertravel.com/tips-romania-
     warnings-dangers-stay-safe/.

"Viscri 125." *Romania*,
     romaniatourism.com/hotels/hotel-
     viscri125.html.